Cooper's Hawk Courtship Display

SUSAN BRANDT GRAHAM, MD, PhD

DEDICATION

To those who know they have been given an extraordinary gift
from Nature when allowed through serendipity to observe something
they never could have planned.

CONTENTS

1 INTRODUCTION

Cooper's hawks are abundant in New Mexico. Once thought to be averse to city life, this highly adaptable hawk has found city life quite comfortable, under the right set of circumstances. The so-called "urban forest" of the Northeast Heights section of Albuquerque, New Mexico, USA, has one of the highest concentrations of Cooper's hawks found anywhere in the US. The established conifers make not only good nesting spots, but good hiding spots from which to lie in wait for the smaller birds that come to the feeders placed by residents. The abundant feeders are virtual cafeterias for these and other birds that prey on smaller birds, such as roadrunners and sharp shinned hawks.

I do have feeders, and enjoy the variety of birds that come to my yard. Over the years I have learned to place feeders to make getting smaller birds a little harder for the roadrunners, which are welcome to eat the lizards in my yard. The hawks are a different matter. They are very fast and swoop in no matter where the feeders are, at least in my experience. Birds of prey have to eat and feed their babies too, and I enjoy seeing them. If I see them too often, I'll take the feeders down for a week or two, and let them go search for food elsewhere.

The time about which I am most conflicted is when baby birds and fledglings are about. The parents need extra food to feed the babies, and the babies are so vulnerable. I realize that Nature does not make emotional judgements, but sometimes I cannot help it.

I have a lot of scrub jays who, for years, have come for the peanuts I feed them. In 2014 I had become attached to a fledgling scrub jay, given the nickname "Little Jay." This image of Little Jay is from July 28, 2014:

The Cooper's hawk images in this volume were taken in my yard on August 3, 2014. I was doing laundry when I caught a glimpse of a large bird flying into a neighbor's tall juniper. I grabbed my camera, and took a few images starting at 1:57pm. But the hawk was really quite well hidden deep in the branches of the juniper, and I came back in to finish laundry, knowing I did not have any good images.

Around 2:50pm I heard the scrub jays making even more noise than is usual for them, distress noises, and I worried about Little Jay in particular. Knowing the hawk had been there, I hoped that maybe I could distract it unless the damage had already been done.

The hawk was in the same tree, but had moved to a spot where I could see it better. I began to photograph, not knowing what had become of Little Jay. I gradually moved closer, up to the point at which the hawk appeared it might fly. For the next few minutes, I almost forgot about what had drawn me outside. Although time seemed to have stood still, the images in the next chapter were recorded between 2:52pm to 2:56pm.

2 COOPER'S HAWK DISPLAY

This beautiful Cooper's hawk is an immature male. When he began his display, I took it to be some type of territorial display because I had gotten too close. I think I briefly considered moving back a little, but the hawk's behavior was too fascinating; I was frozen in place. I have subsequently read that during the nesting season here in Albuquerque, the hawks will dive bomb visitors to city parks in which they have nests. People are advised to take umbrellas with them to lessen the chance of hawk bombings. I did not know about that at the time, and I am just as happy that I didn't. In this case, ignorance was bliss, although I generally am a firm believer that ignorance is dangerous.

After learning more about Cooper's hawk behavior, I realize now this was a type of courtship display. This immature male may have mistaken the long lens for a big bird beak, although I do not know that. Even if he did, the courtship display may not have been because he found it attractive, but it may have been a response to self-preservation. Young male Cooper's hawks live in a precarious position. The females are roughly one-third larger than the males, one of the largest amounts of sexual dimorphism found in hawks. According to the Cornell Lab of Ornithology:

> Life is tricky for male Cooper's Hawks. As in most hawks, males are significantly smaller than their mates. The danger is that female Cooper's Hawks specialize in eating medium-sized birds. Males tend to be submissive to females and to listen out for reassuring call notes the females make when they're willing to be approached.

Regardless, the typical bowing, "mooning," full feather displays and other aspects are seen here. I felt honored to observe it.

Image 1

Image 2

Image 3

Image 4

Image 5

Image 6

Image 7

Image 8

Image 9

Image 10

Image 11

Image 12

Image 13

Image 14

Image 15

Image 16

Image17

Image 13

Image 19

Image 20

Image 21

Image 22

Image 23

Image 24

Image 25

Image 26

Image 27

Image 28

Image 29

Image 30

Image 31

Image 32

3 SERENDIPITY

Photographing this remarkable Cooper's hawk display is nothing I could have planned ahead of time. I had seen the hawk about an hour earlier, but he was well hidden in a large juniper tree where I could not photograph him. I had gone back inside the house to complete weekend chores.

About an hour later the scrub jays were making more noise than usual, and they sounded distressed. I had become fond of a little fledgling scrub jay and I thought maybe the hawk had gotten the little fledgling. My camera was handy at the door, because with the hawk hanging around, I thought I might get a chance to photograph him. Never in my wildest imagination did I dream I would witness something like this display, let alone photograph it. The entire event was over in four minutes, and at the time I was not even certain what I had seen. I did know I had had an intense personal encounter with the hawk. Reading and going back through the images months later allowed me to understand those four minutes a little better.

Little Jay was unharmed, and I believe remains part of an extended family group of scrub jays that comes to eat peanuts on a regular basis.

Nature presents some remarkable happenings, often at the most unexpected times. May you find many serendipitous moments that keep you in awe as you travel through this world.

ABOUT THE AUTHOR

Susan Brandt Graham is an award winning photographic artist offering a unique view into the creative feminine mind. Formally trained as a social anthropologist (PhD), and board certified in Obstetrics and Gynecology (MD), she has taught Anthropology at the university level and had a private Ob-Gyn practice until retiring from clinical medicine. Living in the "Land of Enchantment," she is never at a loss for photographic subjects. Photo essays and conceptual photography are currently her major interests.

"Cooper's Hawk Courtship Display" documents a rarely photographed in-the-trees display. This volume is the first in the series, "As Seen in New Mexico…"

In "Seeing Color Colorblind," Graham uses the art and technology of digital photography to unlock the fascinating world seen through the eyes of her son and father, both with severe red color deficiencies. Intrigued since the early 1970's with how the two of them could watch a football game on a black and white television and discuss "the blue team and the yellow team," she solved the mystery as she worked on "seeing color colorblind." She continues the exploration of the phenomena of color deficient vision.

"Persephone's Choice: Every Woman's Dilemma" combined Graham's background in social anthropology and medicine with conceptual portraiture to discuss "being female."

Visit her Amazon Author Page at
http://amazon.com/author/grahamsusanbrandt or
http://amzn.to/1OSgSQv
and her websites at
http://susanbgraham.com
http://susanbgraham.com/blog
http://seeingcolorblind.com
She may be contacted by e-mail at
SusanBrandtGraham@gmail.com

www.ingramcontent.com/pod-product-compliance
Lightning Source LLC
Chambersburg PA
CBHW050756290526
45792CB00008B/2205